HABITATS

SEAS AND OCEANS

EWAN MCLEISH

Wayland

HABITATS

Coasts
Deserts
Forests
Grasslands
Islands

Mountains
Polar Regions
Rivers and Lakes
Seas and Oceans
Wetlands

Cover: Underwater life around a coral reef in Indonesia.

Title page: A great white shark cruises menacingly through the water.

Contents page: Fishing boats on the beach at Kerala in India.

Series editor: Rosemary Ashley
Book editor: Paul Bennett
Series designer: Malcolm Walker

First published in 1996 by
Wayland (Publishers) Limited
61 Western Road, Hove
East Sussex, BN3 1JD, England

British Library Cataloguing in Publication Data
McLeish, Ewan
    Seas and Oceans. - (Habitats series)
    I. Title II. Series
    574.92

ISBN 0-7502-1491-0

Typeset by Kudos Editorial and Design Services
Printed and bound in Italy by L.E.G.O. S.p.A., Italy

CONTENTS

Chapter 1. Unknown Lands 4

Chapter 2. How the Oceans Were Born 8

Chapter 3. Adapting to Life at Sea 16

Chapter 4. Understanding the Oceans 18

Chapter 5. Habitats for All...26

Chapter 6. Harvesting the Seas 34

Chapter 7. Reaching the Limits.................................40

Chapter 8. Turning the Tide 43

Glossary 46

Books to Read and Further Information 47

Index 48

1. UNKNOWN LANDS

Seas and oceans occupy nearly three-quarters of the earth's surface, and yet we know very little about them. Their great depth, sheer size and power make it difficult to explore them, and because of this they remain 'unknown lands'.

Mountains beneath the ocean

The landscape beneath the ocean is as spectacular as that on dry land. There are mountain ranges the size of the Himalayas rising up from the ocean bed, and trenches so deep that over a tonne of water presses down on every square centimetre. There is a current, called the Gulf Stream, that carries relatively warm water from the seas off Mexico across the Atlantic Ocean to the coast of Norway, where it stops the sea from freezing. And there are waves, created by earthquakes on the ocean bed, that are over 70 metres high and travel at 725 kph.

Below A map showing the world's seas and oceans.

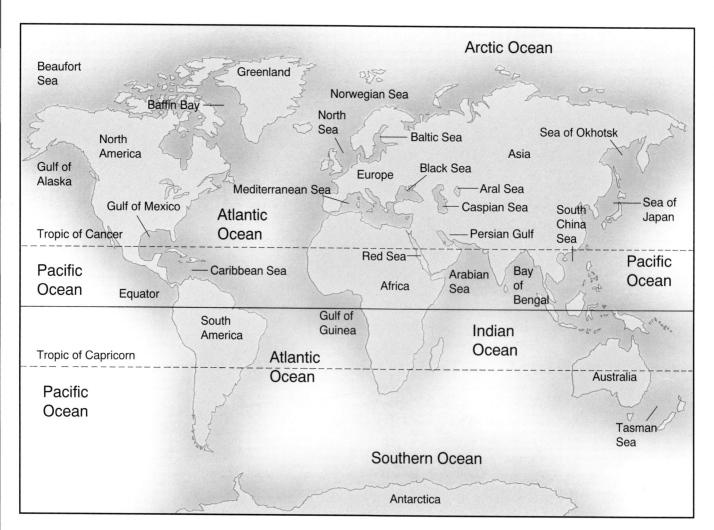

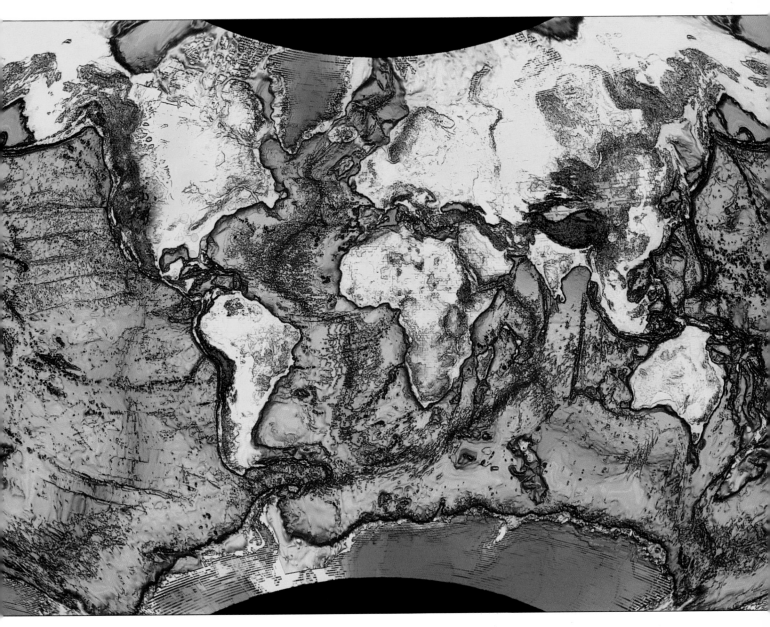

Ocean facts

- *The largest ocean in the world is the Pacific. It represents nearly 46 per cent of the world's oceans and covers over 166 million square kilometres – about sixteen times the area of Europe. Its average depth is 3,939 metres.*
- *The deepest part of the ocean is the Marianas Trench in the Pacific. It is 10,915 metres deep. A solid metal object dropped into the water would take over an hour to reach the bottom.*
- *The highest submarine mountain lies in the Tonga Trench between Samoa and New Zealand. It rises to 8,690 metres – just a little shorter than Mount Everest – and is still 365 metres below the surface.*
- *The highest recorded wind-generated sea wave was 34 metres.*
- *The greatest current is the Antarctic Circumpolar Current. It has a width of between 300 and 2,000 kilometres and flows at a leisurely 0.75 kph.*

This map shows the features of the sea-bed. The shallowest areas are coloured green and the deepest parts are shown in blue. (The continental shelf and low-lying land are shown in yellow. Higher parts of the land are in red and brown.)

Left The whale shark is the world's largest fish. Despite its huge size, this shark is entirely harmless to humans, feeding on small fish and shrimps.

Life beneath the sea

The sea is the largest habitat on earth. It supports a greater variety of life than the tropical rainforests, ranging from tiny plankton to giant whales. Marine creatures can be found everywhere, from the utter darkness of the deepest ocean trenches to the sunlit surface waters.

Below The Spanish shawl, a type of mollusc found off the coast of California in the USA. The brightly coloured filaments are gills and warn enemies that it is unpleasant to eat.

Marine record breakers
• *The largest animal to have ever inhabited the earth is the blue whale, which grows up to a length of 34 metres and weighs up to 190 tonnes. Whales and dolphins are mammals, not fish, because the females feed their young on their own milk. They also breathe air, and so must come to the surface to take a breath.*
• *The Atlantic giant squid is the largest mollusc in the world. It grows to a length of 15 metres and weighs up to 2 tonnes. It also has the largest eye of any animal in the world – 38 centimetres in diameter!*
• *The largest fish in the world is the whale shark, which grows to a length of 18.5 metres and weighs 43 tonnes.*
• *The smallest fish is the dwarf pygmy goby, which weighs only 4 mg and is found in the Philippines.*
• *The Pacific giant kelp is the longest recorded species of seaweed. It can grow to a length of over 60 metres.*

Oceans of life, oceans in danger

The seas and oceans support thousands of millions of people. More than half the world's population live within 60 kilometres of the shoreline. Many are the world's poorest people, for whom the sea is the only source of food and of their livelihood.

However, humans have used the seas and oceans unwisely, perhaps believing that because they are so huge their resources are limitless. Now we have found that we have been over-fishing for years, particularly in the North Sea and Atlantic Ocean, and have run down fish stocks to the point where strict fishing limits have to be imposed. We have hunted the great whales almost to the point of extinction and only now, after determined efforts by conservationists, are they likely to be safe.

We have treated the sea as a giant waste-bin, perhaps thinking that it can cope with whatever we throw into it. Pollution is now a major hazard in many parts of the sea: oil spills devastate shorelines and traces of DDT, a pesticide banned in many parts of the world, can still be found in shrimps caught in the Antarctic.

We have to protect the oceans – if not they will no longer provide the resources we depend on. But first we have to understand the sea and our relationship with it.

'Stilt' fishermen of Sri Lanka casting their lines at sunset. The sea provides not only a living, but is also a way of life for coastal village people like this.

2. HOW THE OCEANS WERE BORN

Where did the oceans first come from? The most likely explanation is that vapour was created from rocks as the newly formed earth gradually cooled. Over millions of years this vapour became the main part of the earth's atmosphere, gradually forming clouds, and then falling as rain. Hot pools and lakes formed and joined together to become the first oceans about 4,000 million years ago. These oceans were very different to the ones we recognize today.

Right Diagram showing the movement of the continents from 560 million years ago to the present day.

Ancient seas

Can you imagine what it was like 560 million years ago? The seas at that time were warm and shallow and were the only places where life existed: primitive plants, soft feathery corals, segmented worms, giant animals related to crabs and lobsters, called trilobites, and jawless fish, all swarmed in the prehistoric seas and oceans.

Most of the continents as we know them today were grouped together to form a huge mass of land, called Gondwanaland. What is now Europe formed part of a smaller continent, called Baltica, and beyond that, in the primitive Atlantic Ocean, lay North America. But the continents were on the move.

Three hundred million years ago, tropical forests of giant tree-ferns clothed the land, while crocodile-like amphibians and early reptiles hunted in the coastal shallow waters. Scaly fish and gigantic sharks swam in a huge ocean, called Panthalassa, which surrounded a single super-continent, called Pangaea. The trilobites were replaced by crabs and lobsters. Sponges, corals, and stalked starfish, called crinoids, dominated the shallow margins of the sea. But the land was still on the move.

A mere 130 million years ago, Tyrannosaurus rex and Triceratops ruled the land, and fish with bony skeletons now dominated the sea. Pangaea had disintegrated and the shape of today's continents and oceans was becoming recognizable. The Americas were tearing themselves away from Europe and Africa to form the Atlantic Ocean; India split itself from Antarctica and headed north to join Asia, to form the Antarctic and Indian Oceans. As Africa swung towards Europe, part of the new sea was cut off – and the Mediterranean Sea was formed. But the great mass of the old Panthalassa sea remained to form the greatest of our oceans – the Pacific.

Above A fossilized trilobite. The hard shell and jointed legs show that this was an early relative of the crab.

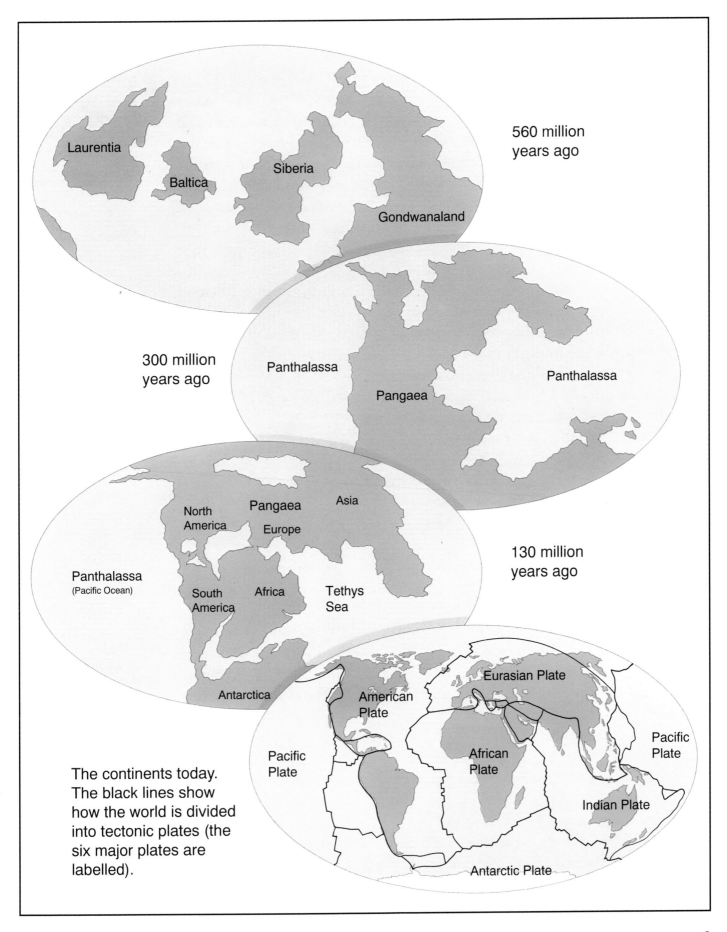

560 million years ago

Laurentia

Baltica

Siberia

Gondwanaland

300 million years ago

Panthalassa

Pangaea

Panthalassa

Pangaea

North America

Europe

Asia

Panthalassa (Pacific Ocean)

South America

Africa

Tethys Sea

Antarctica

130 million years ago

The continents today. The black lines show how the world is divided into tectonic plates (the six major plates are labelled).

Pacific Plate

American Plate

Eurasian Plate

African Plate

Pacific Plate

Indian Plate

Antarctic Plate

Continents adrift

The gradual movement of the continents – less than 10 centimetres a year – is known as continental drift. The interior of the earth is believed to be made up of an inner, molten iron core and an outer stony mantle. The earth has a crust formed from the upper layers of the mantle, which glides on top of this mantle. The crust itself is divided into a number of huge plates, called tectonic plates, on which the continents sit.

When the tectonic plates move apart, new molten rock gradually wells up from the mantle below, becomes solid and forms long mountain ridges. Such a ridge runs along the entire length of the Atlantic Ocean floor from north to south, forming the Mid-Atlantic Ridge. Iceland is situated on top of the ridge and there is regular volcanic activity there.

When two plates come together, one is pushed beneath the other, forming a deep trench. The Tonga Trench to the east of Australia is an example of this. In areas like these, the earth's crust is under great stress and the regions often experience severe earthquakes as well as volcanic activity. When earthquakes occur in the sea-bed, huge tidal waves, or tsunami, can be formed which travel across entire oceans. In 1971 a tsunami of 85 metres was formed, which

A map showing the direction of the world's ocean currents.

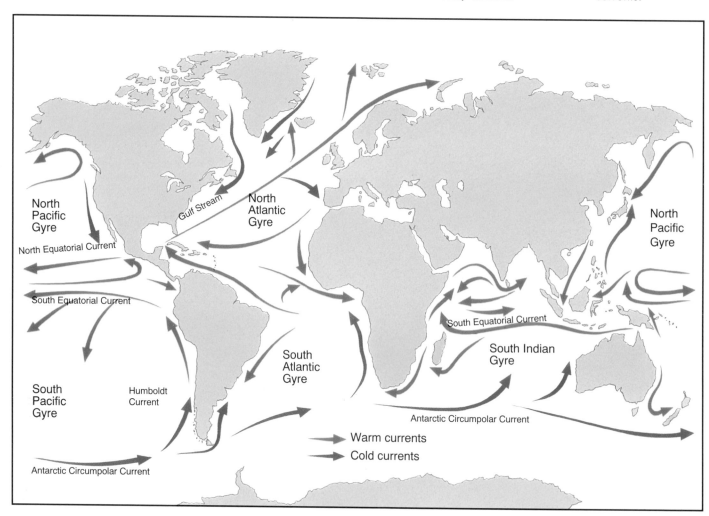

smashed into the coast of Japan, and threw a 750 tonne block of coral 2.5 kilometres.

The continents themselves are made up of a lighter material known as continental crust, and they extend far beyond their coastlines into shallow areas of sea, forming the continental shelf. Then the sea-bed dips down to the ocean floor 4,000 metres below, to the abyss.

Ocean currents

The oceans are constantly on the move, and the wind, tides and rotation of the earth act together to create currents. In each half of the earth, or hemisphere, there is a particular kind of wind. Near the Equator, the trade winds blow the ocean surface waters in a westward direction. Nearer the Poles, the winds come mainly from the west and drive the waters back towards the east. The result is a circular system of currents known as gyres. The Gulf Stream is an example of a gyre. There are similar gyres in the South Atlantic Ocean, the Indian Ocean and the North and South Pacific Ocean.

Closer to the land, currents are mainly created by tidal movements. The tides themselves are caused by the gravitational pull of the moon on the oceans as the earth rotates. Currents have an important influence on the movement of living organisms and the transportation of nutrients throughout the oceans. For example, the long-distance migration of many marine animals, such as turtles and whales, is assisted by the movement of currents.

Early exploration of the Pacific Ocean

People have ventured across the vastness of the oceans since the earliest times. As long ago as 1500 BC, settlers sailed along the great island chains of the South Pacific, probably from New Guinea and Indonesia, using double canoes and outriggers (canoes with stabilizing floats on one or both sides). These people were expert sailors, using the currents and winds, and navigating by the sun and stars, so that by AD 1000, the most remote of the Pacific islands had been settled.

A traditional Indonesian fishing boat with outriggers. Canoes similar to this may have been used to explore the Pacific Ocean.

Rising and falling

The level of our seas does not stay the same. This can be seen when ancient ports or coastal fortifications are found several kilometres inland, or discovered submerged beneath the surface of the sea. During the Ice Ages in particular, sea levels rose and fell dramatically.

At the end of the last Ice Age, about 10,000 years ago, the ice-cap covering northern Europe began to melt. The reduction in weight caused the land beneath to rise, creating a huge freshwater lake, called the Baltic Ice Lake. However, the vast quantity of water released by the melting ice sheets also caused a rise in sea-level, and this lake became flooded by the sea, forming the Baltic Sea. Then, as the land continued to rise, the sea was once more cut off and became fresh water again. Finally, about 4,500 years ago, the sea-level began to rise again and the modern Baltic Sea was formed, with its narrow entrance into the North Atlantic Ocean.

Changes in sea-level are still occurring. Many people are now concerned that the temperature of the earth may be increasing due to the greenhouse effect, thought to be caused by pollution of the earth's atmosphere. There is already some evidence that the ice-caps in the Arctic and Antarctic are melting more each spring. The result could be a rise in sea-level around the world in fifty or a hundred years time of at least a metre. The effects of this on low-lying countries, such as Bangladesh, would be disastrous. Weather patterns around the world may also change, creating deserts where there is now fertile farmland.

Most countries are trying to cut down the amount of greenhouse gases they produce by reducing their use of fossil fuels, such as oil and coal. So far, however, little reduction seems to have been achieved.

Above A small increase in the temperature of our planet could start the melting of the ice-caps of the North and South Poles, flooding many parts of the world.

Land, sea and air

We might think of the seas and oceans as being separate from other parts of the earth. In fact, they have a great influence on the atmosphere and on the land, while they, in turn, affect the seas and oceans. For example, the great oceans help to control the temperature, warming the air in winter and cooling it in the summer.

A tropical storm lashes the coast and tears at the fronds of palm trees lining the beach. Storms are both sudden and violent in tropical areas.

Over millions of years, the flow of rivers has transported enormous quantities of dissolved minerals, particularly sodium chloride (salt) from the land into the oceans. These minerals give sea-water its special properties, which allowed life to develop on the planet. Now the land has other, less beneficial, effects on the sea, as pollution from farming, for instance, finds its way to the sea.

The sea also acts as a natural store for gases in the atmosphere, storing vast quantities of oxygen and carbon dioxide (a greenhouse gas). The algae in the upper water of the oceans take in carbon dioxide during a process called photosynthesis (see page 17). Although much of this gas returns to the atmosphere as the algae 'breathe', some of the carbon is stored in the bodies of the algae. When they die and sink to the sea-bed, the carbon is 'locked away' for thousands of years. In this way algae are important in the control of the greenhouse effect.

Living in salt-water
Although all life began in the sea, living in sea-water is not easy. Most of the sea is actually pitch black as sunlight does not penetrate much below

Two manta rays glide through a clear sea. The flaps at the side of the head help guide shrimp and plankton into the huge mouth.

Turtle tears and shark steaks

When out of the water, marine turtles often look as though they are crying – this is really concentrated salt water being removed by glands around the eyes. Sharks and rays prevent their body water leaking out into sea-water by retaining large amounts of the waste product, urea, increasing the concentration of their body fluids and preventing osmosis. This is why shark meat is very bitter and must be soaked in fresh water many times before it is fit to eat!

A green turtle 'crying'. The 'tears' are made up of unwanted salt being lost from the body. They also help to clear the turtle's eyes of sand when it is on land.

100 metres. This makes it impossible for plants to grow below this depth as they need light for growth and life. Large areas of the oceans are also very poor in nutrients and this makes them rather like deserts in the sea.

Salt water itself is difficult for animals to survive in. The fluids in most marine animals and plants tends to 'leak' out of their bodies into the more salty sea-water in a process known as osmosis. So although they are surrounded by liquid, holding on to their own body fluids is quite a problem. Different animals and plants cope with this problem in different ways, usually by 'pumping out' salt through special cells or glands.

But sea-water also has many properties that are beneficial to life. It supports the bodies of tiny, single-celled animals and the soft bodies of larger organisms, such as jelly fish and sea cucumbers. The great whales would suffocate if much of their enormous weight was not supported by sea-water. Most importantly, sea-water contains all the nutrients necessary to support plant-life, and this plant-life is the foundation for life on earth.

3. ADAPTING TO LIFE AT SEA

Scuba divers are able to survive under the sea because they have tanks of compressed air strapped to their backs, which allow them to breathe as normal. Their movement is aided by large fins attached to their feet, and they can control their buoyancy (the ability to float or rise in the sea) by means of a jacket into which they can pump or remove air.

Fish do not need all this equipment. A barracuda, for example, can match the movement of a scuba diver with a flick of its powerful, striped body. It can get its oxygen directly from the water, and can change its buoyancy and depth by tiny changes to a bladder inside its body. It need never come to the surface.

Like all marine organisms, a barracuda is superbly designed for living in the sea. It is a powerful hunting animal or predator, which relies on speed, well-developed senses, and a spectacular set of teeth to survive. Of course, not all marine animals live in this way. Just as on land, there are plenty of plant-eating animals, too.

Above A school of barracuda on the look out for food. Larger barracuda tend to hunt singly rather than in shoals like this.

Undersea gardens

Animals are not the only living things that can adapt to life in the sea. The vast majority of marine plants are algae. On land they are small and restricted to damp habitats. In the sea they are in their element.

Algae are well suited to life in the ocean. They do not have the woody stems of flowering plants, such as shrubs and trees, because the sea-water supports them instead. The sea allows them to grow to lengths, and even shapes, similar to land plants. It contains all the nutrients they need to grow.

Most seaweeds are anchored to rocks or other surfaces by means of a knotty holdfast that literally digs into the stone to form an anchor. It is not a root because it does not absorb nutrients or water as the roots of flowering plants do. There are other types of algae, however, which do not need holdfasts. They are the tiny floating algae that form the basis of all life in the sea – the phytoplankton.

Above Lobsters are among the largest and most powerful of crustaceans. This diver has found this lobster in a kelp bed.

A knot-like holdfast allows this brown seaweed to attached itself securely to rocks on the sea-bed.

The changing colour of seaweed
Like most plants, seaweeds need to absorb sunlight in order to manufacture food (carbohydrates) from carbon dioxide and water. This process is called photosynthesis. Because of their need for sunlight, seaweeds are limited to fairly shallow water. But light changes as it travels through water, with its different colours gradually being cut out. This affects the colour of seaweed found at different depths. Near the surface and on the shore, green seaweeds are found. Deeper down can be found brown seaweeds, such as wracks and kelps. Deepest of all, where light conditions are poor, are the red and blue seaweeds.

4. UNDERSTANDING THE OCEANS

A diver and a large grouper have a close encounter off Queensland in Australia. It is easy to forget that another diver has to be there to capture the scene on film.

Exploring beneath the waves

Throughout history, humans have attempted to explore the sea. But it was not until 1660 that the first successful piece of diving equipment, the diving bell, was invented. It had an open bottom and was equipped with a supply of air carried in weighted barrels, which were sent down alongside it.

At the beginning of the nineteenth century, the diving suit and helmet were invented, allowing a diver to work underwater with the air being supplied through a tube from the surface. During the twentieth century, various designs were developed to allow the diver to be free of a long air tube, and in 1943 the Frenchman, Jacques Cousteau, invented the self-contained underwater breathing apparatus, or scuba. This consisted of a cylinder of highly compressed air attached to a special valve, which allowed the diver to breathe underwater easily.

Divers cannot safely go much deeper than 100 metres because of the enormous pressure on their bodies from the sea. Underwater craft or submersibles can go much deeper. In 1934, two explorers descended to 1,000 metres in a heavy, steel ball-like submersible, called a bathysphere. It was lowered on a cable from a ship. Later versions, known as bathyscaphs, were independent of surface ships, having their own propulsion and air supply. In 1960, scientists in the submersible, *Trieste,* reached the ocean bed of the Marianas Trench, at nearly 11,000 metres.

Information about the sea can be obtained in other ways. Underwater cameras, sometimes mounted on remote-controlled submersibles, can reveal animals and plants from the deepest abyss. Echo-sounding (sonar), which measures the time taken for a pulse of sound to echo back from a solid object, is used to determine the shape of the sea-bed or the presence of wrecks or even shoals of fish. Other instruments measure temperature, pressure, current and salinity (saltiness of the water). Dredges and grabs can obtain samples of sediment and organisms from the sea-bed for analysis.

A submersible begins its descent to nearly 1,000 metres, taking tourists to view deep sea life in the Caribbean.

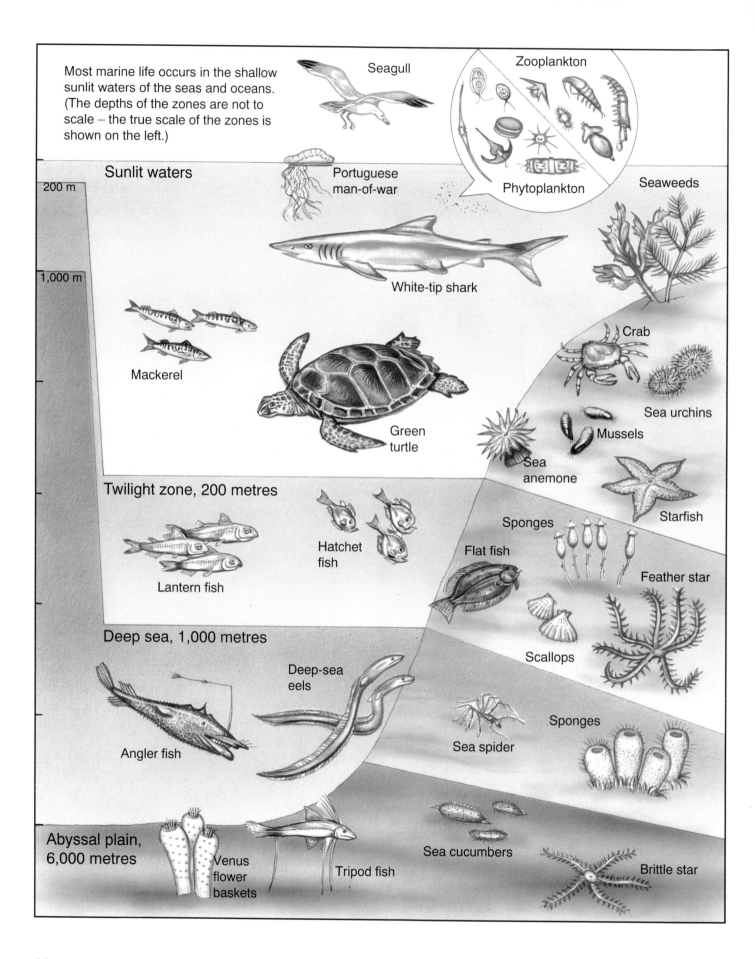

Most marine life occurs in the shallow sunlit waters of the seas and oceans. (The depths of the zones are not to scale – the true scale of the zones is shown on the left.)

Seagull

Zooplankton

Phytoplankton

Sunlit waters

200 m

1,000 m

Portuguese man-of-war

Seaweeds

White-tip shark

Crab

Sea urchins

Mackerel

Mussels

Green turtle

Sea anemone

Starfish

Twilight zone, 200 metres

Sponges

Flat fish

Hatchet fish

Feather star

Lantern fish

Deep sea, 1,000 metres

Scallops

Deep-sea eels

Sponges

Sea spider

Angler fish

Abyssal plain, 6,000 metres

Venus flower baskets

Sea cucumbers

Tripod fish

Brittle star

20

A diagram to show how marine life changes with depth (the creatures shown are not to scale). Living things have adapted to every part of the ocean.

A journey into the deep

If you took an imaginary journey in the *Trieste* to the bottom of the ocean, you would see an ever-changing pattern of life as you descended.

On the surface itself you would see floating animals, such as the Portuguese man-of-war, a relative of sea anemones and jelly-fish. Near the surface would be animals that depend on the well-lit upper waters – shoals of anchovies feeding on the plentiful plankton, and shoals of silver and grey mackerel chasing the anchovies, for example. You would see large predators, such as sharks and marlin, patrolling beneath the waves looking for prey.

At about 200 metres is the twilight zone. Here, fish are less common, and many are coloured scarlet and black so that they can swim unnoticed in the poorly lit waters. At depths as great as 1,000 metres, large animals might still

Above A deep-sea angler fish uses a worm-like lure to entice a fish within reach of its waiting jaws, which can engulf prey almost its own size.

be seen in the submersible's searchlights, such as the 25-metre sperm whale pursuing its prey, the giant squid.

Below 1,000 metres no light penetrates from the surface, and yet you would see tiny pin-points of light. Called bioluminescence, the light is produced by chemicals in the skin of animals and used to attract prey or a mate. Many of the animals are transparent as they have no need for coloration in the darkness. There are many fish with huge jaws, capable of swallowing prey as large as themselves.

At a depth of 6,000 metres, the weight of water pressing on the submersible is thousands of tonnes. At this depth, living things exist at near zero temperatures, feeding on the dead and dying plants and animals that fall in a slow, constant rain on to the ocean floor. Giant brittle starfish and sea cucumbers crawl over the thick sediments, and tripod fish pick their way daintily over the soft surface on leg-like fins.

Phytoplankton

In the open sea there are vast numbers of microscopic algae, or phytoplankton, floating in the upper regions of the oceans. They are the grass of the sea, and the animals, or zooplankton, that feed on them are also tiny – between the size of a flea and a mosquito. Feeding on the zooplankton are larger, carnivorous planktonic animals, growing up to 10 centimetres in length.

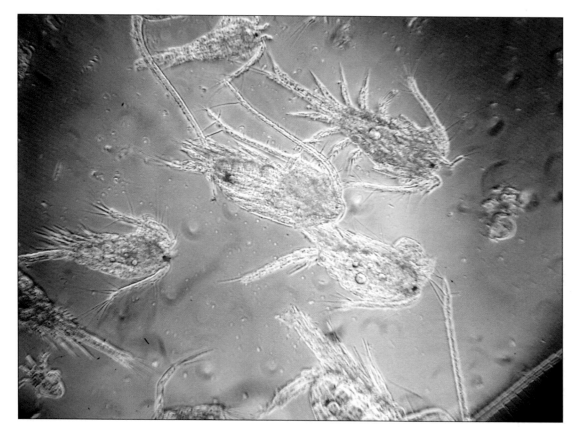

Marine zooplankton. These microscopic animals are related to shrimps.

Many of these animals have evolved extraordinary ways of capturing their smaller prey involving complicated filters and fans. One type of salp, a primitive, barrel-shaped animal, produces a curtain of mucus to catch its prey. When the smaller plankton become caught in it, the salp eats the whole thing, mucus and all.

Some of the larger zooplankton are more active hunters, for example, the arrow worm, which pursues and captures other zooplankton in its jaws. The most abundant of the zooplankton, however, are the crustaceans, shrimp-like creatures which feed by filtering phytoplankton through specially adapted appendages (limbs) mounted with fan-like hairs.

This salp is almost transparent. It feeds on smaller plankton by pumping water through its body, drawing in even smaller organisms which are trapped in the gills which can be seen near the centre of the body.

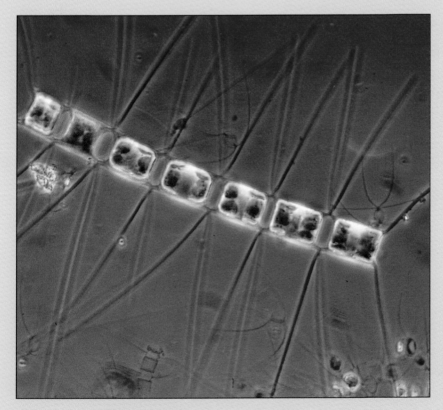

Fantastic shapes

The smallest of the phytoplankton are the diatoms and dinoflagellates. Despite their microscopic size, they are some of the most beautiful of all plants. Their single-celled bodies are supported by an external skeleton made largely of a material called silica. Often this is fashioned into fantastic shapes, perhaps as a way of helping the plants to float or making them less attractive to eat.

Diatoms are a type of phytoplankton and can only be seen under a microscope. The green areas in this diatom contain a material called chloroplasts, which enable these tiny plants to make food through photosynthesis.

The food chain

As on the land, all life in the sea depends on each other in some way for survival in a structure called the food chain. The vast swarms of phytoplankton and zooplankton form the main diet of small fish (such as anchovies and sand eels), which fall prey to larger animals (such as herring, cod and squid). These will be hunted in turn by sea birds (such as gannets and cormorants) and top predators (such as seals, killer whales and sharks). One group of animals, however, misses out several links in this food chain. The great whales, basking sharks, whale sharks and manta rays feed directly on zooplankton itself, or on the small fish that are next in the food chain, such as caplin.

Migrations

Like birds, many marine animals take part in migrations – seasonal journeys from one area to another to make the best use of the available food or breeding sites, for example.

Most fish migrate to spawning grounds to breed. These are usually coastal areas where the water is warm and shallow and there is an abundance of zooplankton to eat. Once the young fish have hatched they travel to a nursery area, usually drifting with the main currents, and later join the adults in their main feeding grounds, perhaps hundreds or even thousands of kilometres from where they were spawned. When mature, the fish will make the difficult journey back to the same grounds to repeat the cycle.

The young eels or elvers of the common eel migrate from the Sargasso Sea to the freshwater rivers of Europe. As adults they will return to the Sargasso Sea to spawn.

The green turtle migrates between its feeding grounds off Brazil to its nesting site on the sandy beaches of the tiny Ascension Islands in the mid-Atlantic Ocean. The grey whale travels each year from its feeding grounds in the Bering Sea in the North Pacific Ocean to breed in the warmer, but less rich, tropical waters off the coast of California (the new-born whales would not survive long in the icy northern seas). The round trip is 16,000 kilometres.

Even planktonic animals migrate, but on a daily basis. At dusk, the zooplankton moves upwards to feed in relative safety on the rich phytoplankton near the surface. During the day it sinks down to darker, safer regions.

Two humpback whales feeding. These whales often co-operate while feeding, releasing a circular 'net' of bubbles underwater which traps small fish in its centre.

It's all done with fringes

The so-called baleen whales, such as blue and fin whales, do not have teeth. Instead they have a row of plates of horn-like material (baleen) with fine fringes along the inner edge hanging from the roof of the mouth. The whale feeds by swimming through a cloud of plankton or krill (small, shrimp-like creatures) with its mouth open. Closing its mouth, the whale then raises its tongue, forcing the food-laden water through the filtering curtain of the plates, while water is expelled from the sides of the mouth. Each mouthful yields about a kilogramme of food, but during the day a whale may consume over 2 tonnes of krill.

5. HABITATS FOR ALL

Sessile animals

A great many animals are not found swimming in the open ocean, but remain attached to rocks or seaweed for most of their lives. Others are adapted to life on the sea-bed and find their food and shelter there.

Animals that are attached to the same spot are called sessile animals, and many have developed sophisticated and often beautiful mechanisms for making sure that their food comes to them. Many of these animals are filter feeders. Their limbs or appendages set up currents in the water to waft particles of food towards them. Other limbs have evolved into nets or filters, straining out the food as the water passes through them. They absorb oxygen at the same time.

Sea snails graze over rocks or sand, scraping up algae and other material with a file-like mouthpiece called a radula.

A fan worm extends a whorl of tentacles from its protective case. The fan extracts oxygen and food from the water.

Getting around
Whether sessile or not, almost all of the animals of the sea-bed have a stage of life that allows them to be carried over large distances. After hatching, the larvae are unrecognizable as the animals they will eventually become, living for a time in the drifting plankton before they eventually settle on the sea-bed. Where they settle will depend on the right conditions being available – barnacle larvae will only choose areas of bare rock between colonies of adults, for example.

Other molluscs, such as whelks, are active hunters, using the radula to bore into the shells of clams, oysters and mussels. Sea urchins scrape over rocks using a ring of teeth controlled by a complicated set of muscles.

More active than any of these, however, are the crabs and lobsters – bold, armoured predators and scavengers that clamber over the rocks in search of food. But even the well-armed crab is no match for another predator of the sea-bed – the highly intelligent and powerful octopus.

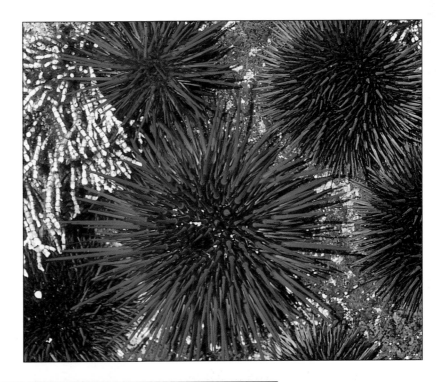

Above Sea urchins in a tidal pool. They graze over the rocks using their ring of teeth.

Left Like an underwater cat, a common octopus pounces on its prey, a luckless crab.

Left A blue-spotted stingray. It has a poisonous spine on its tail which it uses to defend itself. The smaller fish are cleaner wrasse, which feed on parasites on the ray's body.

The sea-bed

Sand or mud is an ideal habitat in which to burrow, either for safety or to wait for prey. Crabs can be found here, just showing two stalked eyes protruding above the surface. Heart urchins burrow about 15 centimetres into the sand using their tube feet. Razor shells can be spotted by the tell-tale 'keyhole' on the surface produced by the siphon (tube) through which they draw water. Meanwhile flat-fish, such as plaice and flounder, and skates and rays (relatives of sharks), cruise over the sand looking for burrowing animals to eat.

Amazing metamorphosis

When young, the plaice looks like a 'normal' fish, but as it matures, one of its eyes 'migrates' to join the other on one side of its head. At the same time the fish starts to swim on its side and its body becomes flattened, adapting the fish for an existence on the sea-bed. Pigments (substances in the skin that produce colour) allow the plaice to match its sandy background.

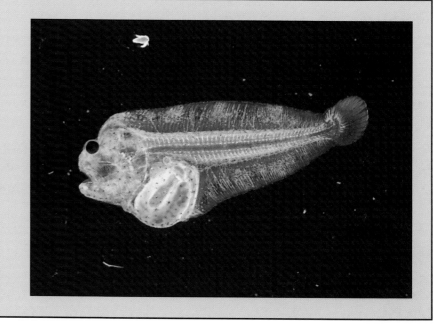

A ten-day-old sole larva. Its body is beginning to change shape.

Coral reefs

Corals occur in all the seas of the world, but they only form reefs in waters that have an average temperature of at least 21°C. A reef-building coral starts life as a tiny planktonic larva that settles in warm, shallow water. The larva develops into a polyp, a small anemone-like creature which feeds by filtering out plankton in the water and grows by developing other individuals from its body. Soon there is a colony of hundreds of separate polyps, living in a common skeleton which forms the reef. As the colony grows upwards and outwards, the original members die, but their internal skeletons of calcium (a substance found in bones and teeth) survive. So the reef itself grows until it may be tens of metres high and hundreds, or even thousands, of kilometres long.

Because of their rock-like and craggy structure, coral reefs make ideal habitats for a variety of other animals. Sponges, filter-feeding crustaceans, boldly marked tiger cowries (a type of marine snail), brittle starfish and sea urchins all live on coral reefs. Sea cucumbers (related to starfish) munch on dead coral and shells, reducing them to a fine, white sand.

Polynesian islands in the Pacific Ocean. The main island is surrounded by a coral reef, called a fringing reef. The water inside the fringing reef is called a lagoon.

An incredible number of dazzling fish swarm around coral reefs. Most are highly adapted to the coral reef habitat. The fish are narrow but have deep bodies, allowing them to slip into crevices when danger threatens. The long-snouted butterfly fish delicately removes individual polyps from the coral, while the large yellow and blue parrot fish gnaws at the coral with its crushing beak. In the larger crevices lurk moray eels.

Coral reefs are self-contained communities of plants and animals, all of which depend on each other in some way for their survival. Such communities are known as ecosystems. Because of their richness, they are an important source of food for many people, particularly in the developing countries and island nations. Reefs also provide the nutrients which support many commercial as well as local fisheries.

But corals are easily damaged. A dragging anchor or fishing net can leave behind a trail of destruction. Scuba divers can damage living coral through thoughtless behaviour, such as hitting the coral with their fins.

A shoal of lyre-tailed goldfish swarm around a coral reef in the Red Sea. The reef provides a habitat for a wide variety of animals and plants.

Collecting coral and the animals that live on it for the tourist trade is also a serious threat to reefs, as is the collecting of fish for sale in pet shops.

But there are more serious dangers. Corals are very sensitive to pollution. Often they grow in areas which attract tourists. Pollution from hotels and other human interference can threaten the habitat. Oil spills are a hazard in areas where there are oil rigs, such as the Red Sea, the Caribbean Sea, and the Persian Gulf.

Corals are also affected by small quantities of silt (particles of mud) in the water, which reduce the amount of light reaching the reef and clog up the filter system of the polyps. Poor agricultural methods leading to soil erosion and waste from mining or quarrying increase the amount of silt entering the sea from rivers. In Thailand, where mining is concentrated on the coast, a number of reefs are literally being smothered to death, while on some tropical islands, coral is mined as a construction material itself.

A glass-bottomed boat tour of the coral reef in Ningaloo Marine Park in Western Australia. Tourists can view the reef without disturbing its inhabitants.

Green lodgers

Reefs would not exist but for algae which live in the tissue of corals and allow the corals to convert calcium in the water into their hard skeletons. These algae require warm temperatures and good light conditions in order to photosynthesize, which is why coral reefs are only found in tropical and sub-tropical waters. The corals get skeletons and the algae get secure homes and plenty of nutrients. This close relationship is known as symbiosis.

Saving the reefs

Some measures are being taken to protect coral reefs. Several countries, such as the USA, Kenya and the Seychelles, now have marine park programmes which emphasize the benefits to tourism and the economy of the protected areas. Other countries, such as Saudi Arabia and Sri Lanka, are just beginning to develop marine parks.

Some reefs, for example, those on the Galapagos Islands, and the Great Barrier Reef off Queensland in Australia, are so important that they have been named World Heritage Sites, and so receive special protection. But even then they may not be safe. After the Second World War (1939–45), a marine snail, the giant triton, that preyed on starfish, was taken from the Great Barrier Reef in large numbers as souvenirs for the tourist trade. This allowed a coral-eating starfish, the crown-of-thorns, to multiply rapidly and devastate some areas of the reef. Now the crown-of-thorns is largely under control.

A crown of thorns starfish straddles a coral head, relentlessly devouring the polyps. Over-collection of its natural predator, the giant triton, allowed this starfish to flourish.

Inland seas

Not all seas are vast open areas. Some, such as the Caspian Sea, are completely enclosed by land. Others have only a narrow outlet to the main oceans, for example, the Mediterranean Sea and the Baltic Sea. These seas often have particular conditions that affect the animals and plants found in them.

The salinity (amount of salt) in inland seas can vary dramatically. For example, where the River Danube enters the Black Sea, the water is quite fresh, but away from the river, the water becomes moderately saline (about half that of the oceans). Below about 200 metres the amount of oxygen in the water is often very low, so few animals can be found below this depth.

Trawling in the Mediterranean Sea. Over-fishing and pollution threatens the fishing industry in many of the world's seas and oceans.

The Mediterranean Sea is connected to the Atlantic Ocean. It contains most of the Atlantic species of fish and about 120 of these are fished commercially. The value of fishing in the Mediterranean is greater than that of any other ocean.

The shrinking sea

The Aral Sea is a large inland sea situated between Kazakhstan and Uzbekistan in Central Asia. After the Second World War, the rivers that fed the sea were diverted to irrigate cotton. Since the rivers no longer flooded the surrounding land, the soil became poor and farmers were forced to use expensive fertilizers and pesticides. Between 1960 and 1990, the area of the sea shrank by 40 per cent. The sea became increasingly saline and polluted. The once thriving fishing industry disappeared, the drinking water became contaminated, and the soil became too salty to grow crops. The fishing port of Muynak is now 48 kilometres inland. Plans are underway to divert water from another river, but it is unlikely that the sea, and the communities it supported, will ever fully recover.

A boat stranded in a sea of sand in the Aral Sea in Central Asia. People created a desert from a once flourishing inland sea.

6. HARVESTING THE SEAS

Humans have depended on the seas and oceans throughout history, first as a source of food and later for their mineral wealth and sources of energy. But we are harming the seas and oceans by over-exploiting them.

Mining

The earliest mineral deposit to be taken from the sea was salt. It was extracted by allowing sea-water to evaporate in pans (shallow pools), leaving a layer of salt crystals behind. Today, the recovery of sand and gravel (aggregates) by dredging is an important mineral industry – only the mining of oil and gas is more important. Aggregates are found close to the shore, and this makes them easy to extract as the water is shallow. The North Sea and Japan are major aggregate extraction sites.

Other minerals which are recovered by dredging include aragonite, phosphate and manganese nodules. Placer deposits (minerals that have been washed into the sea and concentrated on the sea-bed, such as iron, tin, titanium, and zircon) are also extracted by dredging.

Gravel being removed from the shallow sea-bed in St Esjberg Port in Denmark.

Modern oil platforms are built to withstand dreadful weather conditions that might only occur once in a hundred years.

Dredging can affect local currents, which in turn can affect the way in which the sea transports material close to the shore. This may result in the build-up or erosion (wearing away) of beaches along the coast. Mineral extraction can increase the amount of silt in the water, reducing the light and affecting filter-feeding animals, especially corals.

Another group of minerals are extracted in a different way. They are pumped from beneath the sea-bed in liquid form. These include sulphur, potash and oil.

Fossil fuels

Oil is a product of the sea itself, for it formed from the microscopic plants that inhabited the oceans millions of years ago. Drilling techniques have been developed to exploit this resource, and today oil rigs stand in over 330 metres of water and can withstand the harsh conditions of the open sea. The drills themselves can penetrate several kilometres into the continental crust.

Oil and gas are piped ashore where the oil is refined to produce a variety of products, such as kerosene (aviation fuel), petrol, and lubricating oils. It may be transported, either as crude or refined oil, to countries around the world in tankers.

From algae to oil
Many millions of years ago, the seas swarmed with planktonic algae. When these died, they sank to the sea-bed and over time were covered with layers of sand and mud. These gradually became compressed and formed sedimentary rock. The organic (plant) material in the rock decomposed (broke down) to form oil and gas. Oil and gas are called fossil fuels because they were formed from living things which died millions of years ago.

Tidal and wave power

Reserves of oil and gas are not endless. The burning of these fossil fuels produces carbon dioxide, which adds to the problem of global warming. By using the power of tides and waves, a less damaging form of energy is available. Tidal energy is produced by building a barrier or barrage across the mouth of an estuary or inlet. These contain machines called turbines which, when turned by the flow of water, generate electricity. One of these plants is at the mouth of the Rance River in France, which produces 240 megawatts of power, about a quarter of a conventional power station.

Possible sites for future tidal power stations include Turnagain Bay in Alaska, USA, and the Severn Estuary in England. Such proposals are controversial because barriers cause the flooding of tidal mudflats, which are vital feeding grounds for ducks, geese and wading birds.

The technology to extract energy from waves also exists, but full-scale production is a long way off. Other ideas, one involving the use of temperature differences between different layers of water, are also only experimental. The large sums invested in fossil fuels means that these alternatives are not a high priority.

Above The Rance tidal power station near St Malo in France. Despite its potential, tidal power is rarely harnessed.

Fishing

The main fishing areas are found close to land in waters less than 400 metres deep. These include the North Atlantic Ocean, the North Sea, the Barents Sea, the Bering Sea, the Gulf of Alaska, the coastal waters around Japan, and in the Pacific Ocean around China, Malaysia and Peru. As well as commercial operations, fishing also supports thousands of local communities, particularly in the developing countries and on small islands.

But stocks of fish are not limitless. Following the end of the Second World War, improved technology, more powerful boats, bigger nets and rising demand, caused a huge expansion of the world fishing industry. The total catch doubled every ten years, reaching 50 million tonnes a year in the late 1960s. Then, in the early 1970s, it fell. The sea could not support the demand for fish and many major food species in the north-east Atlantic Ocean and North Sea, such as herring and cod, went into serious decline.

The decline in fish stocks has led to a number of international agreements to regulate fishing by putting limits or quotas on the amount of most food species that can be caught. But these quotas are not always kept to and they are difficult to enforce. The minimum size at which different species of fish can be caught is also regulated by setting limits on the mesh size of nets (the size of the open spaces between the net strands). If the mesh size is large enough, fish that are not fully grown can escape, giving them a chance to reach breeding size, and so

The end for a fishing community

In a small fishing community in southern Thailand, local fish stocks have been wiped out by foreign fishing boats. The villagers are forces to dive with their nets into deep, rocky areas where the fishing boats cannot go. They use make-shift diving equipment made from rubber tubing and old generators. Some drown, others suffer from the 'bends' – a sickness caused by returning too rapidly to the surface – and become disabled or die. Soon these fish will be gone too. But fishing is the only way of life the villagers know.

replenish the stock, before they are caught. But there are still problems. For example, in the North Sea, young cod and haddock are trapped in small-meshed nets designed to take smaller fish, such as Norway pout.

The competition between fishing countries is extremely fierce. For example, countries of the European Union (EU) all have access to the waters around Europe, but must observe individual fishing quotas for each country. Because of declining stocks, these quotas may not be reached. The smaller, family fishing businesses, such as those operating from south-west England and southern Ireland, are poorly equipped to compete with the powerful

Fishing boats on Kovalam Beach, in India. Methods of fishing here have not changed significantly for hundreds of years.

deep-sea trawlers of countries such as Spain. Many have gone out of business.

Sometimes there is actual hostility between countries. For example, in 1995 EU fishing boats were accused of over-fishing in the North Atlantic Ocean by Canada, and their boats and nets were held by the Canadian authorities. The Canadians believed that, without tougher regulations, whole fishing communities, such as those in Newfoundland, were threatened.

An alternative to catching fish, is to farm them. Pacific salmon are produced in hatcheries in north-western USA and in Norway, and are then released into the ocean. Salmon are a migratory species and can be caught when they return as adults to spawn. Shellfish, such as oysters, are also cultivated and make up half of all US production. Shrimps are raised in Ecuador, Mexico and Taiwan, and Japan is experimenting by breeding lobsters and crabs.

A new fish-rearing method involves the creation of artificial reefs which attract seaweed, crustaceans and fish. Reefs may consist of rubble or even old tyres. Japan has almost doubled its inshore fishing catch by building 2,500 artificial reefs along its coastline.

Above Fish are vacuumed ashore in a Danish port. Modern fishing methods mean that a single boat can land huge catches.

Whaling

Whaling is an ancient human activity. For example, the Inuit, the native people from North America and Greenland, have always hunted whales for food and fuel. Whale oil has been put to many different uses. Less than thirty years ago, it was still being used as cooking oil or turned into margarine or soap.

As early as the seventeenth century, numbers of slow-moving, inshore species of whale, such as the Greenland right whale or bowhead whale, were severely reduced by whaling in the North Sea. The development in 1760 of brick ovens on board ships, in which the whale blubber (fat) could be converted into oil, meant that whaling boats could travel much further from land, opening up new whaling grounds in tropical areas and in the Antarctic.

In 1864, the invention of a harpoon with an explosive tip, the grenade harpoon, fired from a cannon mounted at the front of a boat, the bow, meant the extinction of some species of whales. In the twentieth century, the boats used to harpoon the whales became faster and easier to steer, and aircraft were used to guide the whaling ships.

Modern factory ships could process entire whales so that whaling fleets could operate almost continuously at sea. An average of 30,000 whales were taken every year until the Second World War. After the war, an attempt was made by many countries to limit whaling and establish sanctuaries. But the limits were impossible to enforce and whale stocks continued to decline. Between 1956 and 1965, a staggering total of 403,490 baleen whales and 228,328 sperm whales were killed.

In 1946, the International Whaling Commission (IWC) was formed in an attempt by the whaling nations to limit whaling and to protect species close to extinction. But it was almost impossible to get all its members to agree on the actions that should be taken. Slowly, certain species of whales were protected, such as the blue whale in 1967, but traditional whaling nations, such as Norway, the USSR and Japan, continued to hunt others. By the early 1970s, only the small minke whale was left in any number.

Perhaps the turning point was public reaction. A number of campaigning organizations, such as Greenpeace, drew attention to the issue of whaling. In 1986, the IWC imposed an indefinite ban on all commercial whaling. This meant that all large-scale whaling would cease for an unknown period, at least until whale stocks had recovered. Limited whaling still continues by some countries for so-called scientific purposes, and some illegal whaling also undoubtedly goes on. Whaling by small island communities who depend on the sea is still allowed.

In 1994, 30 million square kilometres of ocean surrounding Antarctica were designated a whale sanctuary. Now over a third of the world's oceans have hopefully been made safe for whales for all time.

A harpooned minke whale is tied alongside a Japanese whaling ship. Although there is a ban on all commercial whaling, a number of nations are pressing for whaling to be resumed as soon as stocks recover.

7. REACHING THE LIMITS

As well as harvesting the sea, we use it as a dump, either on purpose or 'accidentally'. The sea can cope with a certain amount of pollution, but when its limit is reached, the results can be devastating for the marine environment.

On 24 March 1989, the 300-metre supertanker, *Exxon Valdez*, ran aground on a reef shortly after leaving the port of Valdez, in Alaska. Over 50 million litres of crude oil gushed from her tanks into Prince William Sound, an area rich in marine wildlife and economically crucial to local fishing communities. By the next day, an oil slick of 128 square kilometres was spreading fast.

Above A protective 'boom' is placed around the *Exxon Valdez* as it leaks oil into Prince William sound in Alaska.

High winds hindered efforts to mop up the oil and the company who owned the ship, Exxon, was heavily criticized for responding too slowly to the disaster. Over 35,000 seabirds perished by drowning or starving to death after swallowing oil. Over 100 kilometres of shoreline was devastated and local fisheries were destroyed. Some areas have still not recovered.

Sources of pollution

Perhaps surprisingly, tanker accidents are not the greatest source of oil pollution. Half of all oil pollution comes from the land – from drains,

Left Following the *Exxon Valdez* disaster, high-pressure hoses were used to blast the oil from the rocks of Prince William Sound.

These children are playing near a sewage outfall on North Island in New Zealand. Despite protests, many countries still use the sea for the disposal of raw or only partly treated sewage.

refineries, and pipe-lines, for example – and nearly a third from tankers deliberately washing out their tanks at sea, even though there are now non-polluting (but more expensive) alternatives.

Oil is only one of many pollutants. Three-quarters of the sewage from Britain's coastal towns and cities is discharged raw (untreated) into the sea. Two-thirds of the sewage from the countries bordering the Mediterranean Sea is pumped into the sea. Sewage produces high levels of nutrients near the coast, causing rapid algae growth. Some of the algae produce toxins (poisons) which kill all other organisms. Then, as the algae break down or decompose, oxygen is removed rapidly from the water, causing further damage to marine life. Bathing in water contaminated by sewage causes stomach upsets and ear, eye and skin infections.

Poisonous metals, such as mercury and barium, enter the sea and atmosphere from industrial processes. Four hundred people on the Japanese island of Kyushu died as a result of eating shellfish contaminated by mercury from a processing plant on the coast.

Thousands of chemicals are manufactured annually for industrial and agricultural purposes. Many, such as the pesticide, dieldrin, and the group of chemicals known as PCBs, are highly toxic. When these toxic materials enter the marine environment, they remain there for years, and can be found in animals in the Arctic and Antarctic, and even in rat-tail fish found at a depth of 3,000 metres.

Although the dumping of radioactive waste is now banned, radioactive material still enters the sea from the cooling water of nuclear power stations. The Irish Sea is known as the most radioactive sea in the world, although levels are well below those that are considered unsafe by the authorities.

About 6.4 million tonnes of litter are dumped in the oceans every year, mostly from ships. Even parts of Antarctica and the deep sea-bed are littered with packaging material. Discarded nets and lines kill a million seabirds and 100,000 seals, whales and dolphins every year.

This young cape fur seal has become tangled in a fishing net. It is unlikely to survive.

Toxic Baltic
Inland seas are easily affected by pollution. Unlike the open ocean, their waters are 'trapped' by the land, so the pollution cannot be washed away. In the summer of 1988, a slick of toxic algae more than 10 metres deep and 10 kilometres wide spread along the mouth of the Baltic Sea. More than 200 kilometres of coastline were affected, beaches were closed and millions of fish died. About 100,000 square kilometres of the Baltic's deep water (about half) is now virtually lifeless because of pollution.

8. TURNING THE TIDE

The seas are suffering because of human exploitation. We are now faced with the choice of managing them responsibly or, in effect, letting them die.

Agreeing to work together

The sea has no real boundaries. The pollution of one country will affect other countries. One nation's over-fishing will damage everyone's fish stocks. In 1992, all the world leaders met in Rio de Janeiro in Brazil to agree what measures needed to be taken to manage our effect on the planet. It was called the United Nations Conference on Conservation and Development (UNCED), or the Earth Summit.

The Earth Summit showed it was no longer possible to look just at the conservation of resources. It was necessary to look at people's lives and livelihoods at the same time, that is, at how countries could develop to allow everyone a reasonable standard of life, without damaging the resources on which they depend.

Rubbish left by tourists on the Caribbean coast of Venezuela. People often fail to make a connection between their own actions and the state of the environment.

This is known as sustainability, or sustainable development.

One of the outcomes of the Earth Summit was an 'action agenda' called Agenda 21. It sets out the actions that all countries need to take to make the earth more sustainable as we move into the twenty-first century. The largest single chapter is on the sea. Some of the key actions that all coastal and island countries should take are:

- manage marine and coastal areas together, not as separate environments;
- improve measures to prevent, reduce or control pollution, especially from land-based sources;

- control fishing at sustainable levels, while increasing the potential of living marine resources, for example, making better use of fish caught but not normally eaten;
- carry out research to improve understanding of the marine environment, for example, they should monitor the effects of tourism or farming on pollution or habitat destruction;
- work together to achieve these aims.

But all this will cost a great deal of money. Many of the poorer countries cannot afford the improvements or sacrifices that are necessary. They claim that the richer countries should help pay for them and reduce their own use of resources. Reaching workable solutions will not be easy.

A young girl from the Philippines sells coral and shells from a boat. There are other ways of developing tourism and creating local jobs without endangering wildlife.

Making progress

Since the early 1970s, many international marine agreements have been signed to regulate dumping, forbid the disposal of plastics at sea, and control oil discharges from ships cleaning out their tanks. The countries bordering the Baltic Sea are working together to reduce pollution.

The countries bordering the North Sea have reached agreements to halt the dumping of sewage and industrial material from ships, stop burning toxic wastes at sea, and reduce river pollution. The Mediterranean countries were the first of twelve 'regional seas' to have clean-up programmes. Now 120 countries are involved world-wide.

Some marine sites, such as the Great Barrier Reef, are now designated World Heritage Sites, and receive special protection. Many countries have their own marine nature reserves. Britain has two, Skomer and Lundy islands, but many people argue there should be more. Public awareness of issues, such as marine pollution and whaling, have also been increased, largely due to the activities of environmental organizations. Greater understanding means governments are more likely to take action to protect the seas.

Taking the initiative

Often, real progress comes down to individuals, particularly when they work together. By cutting down our own waste, recycling materials, such as plastics, and disposing of harmful substances responsibly, we can all contribute to the care of our seas. There are also many organizations which encourage young people to become involved in marine projects or which campaign on, for example, whaling or the dumping of chemicals at sea. It does not matter whether you live near the sea or not – everyone is equally responsible.

Take an interest in the sea and learn about it. If you are lucky enough to go on holiday to the coast, take care not to damage marine habitats in any way. Find out how hotels, for example, dispose of their waste. Avoid buying anything, such as shells, that could have come from living animals or plants.

When on the beach look at the 'strand line', where the high tide leaves material washed up by the sea. You will learn a lot about what lives in the sea and also what we dump in it. Respect the sea for its own sake and for what it gives us. In this way we will all learn to protect it.

A wild bottle-nosed dolphin allows itself to be stroked at Monkey Mia in Western Australia. People feel a natural link with the seas – if we understand more about the seas, we can learn to protect them.

GLOSSARY

Algae   Simple plants which do not produce flowers; seaweeds are algae.

Amphibians   Animals that live both on land and in water.

Antarctic   The region around the South Pole.

Aragonite   A material like marble, composed of calcium carbonate.

Arctic   The region around the North Pole.

Communities   Groups of animals and plants that live together in an area.

Conservationists   People who are concerned with the protection of the environment.

Contaminated   Made dirty or impure.

Continents   The earth's large land masses (Asia, Australia, Africa, Europe, North and South America, and Antarctica).

Crustaceans   Animals that have hard shells and jointed legs, such as crabs, lobsters and shrimps.

Currents   Streams of water moving in a certain direction.

Diversity   The variety of living organisms, sometimes known as biodiversity.

Dredging   The mechanical removal of large amounts of material from the sea-bed.

Estuary   The wide, lower part of a river near the sea, where the tide travels.

Evaporate   The change in state of a liquid to a gas or vapour.

Filter feeders   Animals that strain small organisms (plankton or small fish) from the water with hairs or bristles.

Fish stocks   The number of fish available that can be caught.

Food chain   The relationship between different animals and plants in a community, each member of which feeds on another in the chain and is in turn eaten.

Fossil fuels   Fuels, such as gas, coal and oil, that formed from the remains of prehistoric plants and animals.

Gravitational pull   A force exerted by all large bodies, such as planets. The moon's gravity pulls the oceans towards it, creating high and low tides in different parts of the world.

Greenhouse effect   The effect of greenhouse gases trapping some of the sun's heat that would normally escape back into space.

Greenhouse gases   Gases in the atmosphere, such as carbon dioxide and methane, which are causing a rise in temperature over the earth's surface (global warming).

Habitat   The natural home of animals and plants, for example, the sea, wetlands, deserts, or woods.

Ice Ages   Cooler periods when ice sheets covered large areas of the earth's surface.

Irrigation   The artificial watering of plants, for example, by diverting rivers or streams, or the sinking of wells.

Larval stage   The young or juvenile stage in an animal's development (larva) when it usually bears no resemblance to the adult it will become.

Manganese nodules   Lumps of the minerals, manganese and iron oxide, found on the deep sea floor in enormous quantities.

Mantle   The thick, rocky layer of the earth between the crust and the core.

Mollusc   A member of the group of animals that includes snails, scallops, sea slugs and octopuses.

Nutrients   Substances, such as minerals, that plants and animals need for growth and life.

Photosynthesis   The process by which nearly all plants can use sunlight to turn water and the gas, carbon dioxide, into food.

Saline   Containing salt; salty.

Sediment   Material made up of plant remains and silt that sinks and forms a layer on the sea-bed.

Soil erosion   The wearing away of soil by wind or water, usually into rivers or the sea.

Spawning grounds   Areas in which animals, particularly fish, breed and produce eggs.

Sustainable development   Ways in which countries or communities can improve the lives of people without endangering the environment.

Tidal mudflats   Large expanses of mud, alternately exposed and covered by the tide. Many are important feeding sites for water birds.

Trenches   Deep canyons in the sea-bed.

Vapour   Tiny particles of water in the air.

Books to Read and Further Information

Atlas of the Environment by G. Lean and D. Hinrichsen (Helicon Publishing, 1992)
Atlas of the Oceans by M. Bramwell (editor) (Crescent Books, 1990)
The Atlas of the Living World by D. Attenborough, P. Whitehead, P. Moore and B. Cox
   (Weidenfeld and Nicholson, 1989)
The Guiness Guide to Nature in Danger by Noel Simon (Guiness Publications, 1993)
Kingdom of the Deep by C. Wilcox (Boxtree Ltd/Survival Anglia, 1990)
The Living Planet by D. Attenborough (Collins, 1984)
Whales, Dolphins and Porpoises by R. Harrison and M. Bryden (Merehurst, 1989)

If you want to know more about conservation in seas and oceans, write to the following organizations:

Friends of the Earth, 26–28 Underwood Street, London N1 7JQ.
Greenpeace, Canonbury Villas, London N1 2PN.
International Whaling Commission, The Red House, 135 Station Road, Histon,
   Cambridge CB4 4NP.
Marine Conservation Society, 9 Gloucester Road, Ross-on-Wye, Herefordshire HR9 5BU.
Royal Society for the Protection of Birds, The Lodge, Sandy, Bedfordshire SG12 2DL.
Seafish Industry Authority, Seafish House, St Andrews Dock, Hull HU3 4QE.
Surfers against Sewage, The Old Courthouse Warehouse, Wheal Kitty, St Agnes,
   Cornwall TR5 0RE.
WATCH Trust for Environmental Education, The Green, Witham Park, Waterside South,
   Lincoln LN5 7JR.
Whale and Dolphin Society, 19A James Street West, Avon, Bath BA1 2BT.
Worldwide Fund for Nature, Panda House, Weyside Park, Cattershall Lane, Godalming,
   Surrey GU7 1XR.

Picture acknowledgements
Bruce Coleman/Gerald Cubitt contents page, /Jens Rydell 8, /David Hughes 15, /Dr Frieder Sauer 17(left), 22, 23(both), /Jane Burton 25(top), /Dr Frieder Sauer 26, /Jane Burton 27, /Kim Taylor 28(bottom), /Carl Roessler 32, /Gerald Cubitt 37; Environmental Picture Library/John Novis 36, /Steve Morgan 39, /Henk Merjenburgh 40, /Rob Franklin 41; Eye Ubiquitous/Paul Bennett 31; Rex Features 40(top); Science Photo Library/BP/NRSC 5; Still Pictures/Norbert Wu 6(both), /Mark Edwards 11, /Yves Lefevre 14, /Norbert Wu 18, /Yvres Lefevre 19, /Norbert Wu 21, /Mark Cawardine 25(bottom), /Michel Gunther 33(top), /Eastlight 33(bottom), /Mark Edwards 38, /Julio Etchart/Reportage 43; Tony Stone/Mike Steverns cover, /Jeff Rotman title page, /Roy Giles 7, /Ken Biggs 13, /Mike Steverns 16, /Jeff Rotman 17(right), 24, /Marc Chamberlain 28(top), /Jean-Marc Truchet 29, /Art wolfe 42, /Paul Chesley 44; Wayland Picture Library 35; ZEFA/Goebel 12, 27. Maps and diagrams on pages 4, 9, 10, 20 by Peter Bull.

INDEX

Numbers in **bold** refer to photographs

abyss 11
Africa 8
algae 14, 16, 17, 22, 26, 31, 35, 42
ancient seas 8
  life in 8
  trilobite 8, **8**
angler fish **21**
Antarctic 7, 8, 12, 38, 39, 42
Aral Sea 33, **33**
Arctic 12, 42
Atlantic Ocean 4, 7, 8, 10, 11, 12,
  33, 36, 37
Australia 10, **18**, **31**, 32, **45**

Baltic Sea 12, 32, 42, 44
barracuda 16, **16**
bioluminescence 22
Black Sea 32

Caribbean Sea 31
Caspian Sea 32
continental drift 8, **9**, 10
continental shelf 11
coral reefs 29–31, **29**, **30**, **31**, 32
  damage to 30, 31, 32, 35
  life on 29–30, 32, **32**
  polyps 29, 30, 31
  protection of 32
Cousteau, Jacques 18
crabs 8, 27, **27**, 28

diving equipment 16, 18
dolphins 6, 42, **45**
dredging 34–5, **34**

Earth Summit 43
eels 25

fan worm **26**
filter feeders 26, 29, 35
fishing **3**, 7, **7**, 30, 33, **33**, 36–9,
  37, **38**, 43–4
  artificial reefs 38
  fish farms 38
  over-fishing 7, 36, 37, 38, 44
  quotas 36–7

global warming 12, 36
Great Barrier Reef 32, 44
greenhouse effect 12, 14
Greenpeace 39
Gulf Stream 4, 11
gyres 11

holdfasts 17, **17**

Ice Age 12
Iceland 10
Indian Ocean 8, 11

Japan 11, 34, 36, 38, 39
jelly fish 15, 21

kelp 6, **17**
krill 25

lobsters 8, **17**, 27

manta rays **14**, 24
marine parks **31**, 32, 44–5
Mediterranean Sea 8, 32, 33, **33**, 41
metamorphosis 28, **28**
migration 11, 24–5, **25**
mining 31, 34
  fossil fuels 12, 31, 35, **35**, 36
  sand and gravel 34, **34**

North Sea 7, 34, 36, 37, 38, 44
Norway 4, 37, 38, 39

oceans **4**
  currents 4, 5, **10**, 11
  depth of 4, 5, **5**
  origins of 8, **9**
  size of 4, 5
octopus 27, **27**

Pacific Ocean 5, 6, 8, 11, 36
Persian Gulf 31
photosynthesis 14, 17, 23, 31
plankton 6, 21, 23, 25, 26, 29, 35
  phytoplankton 17, 22, 23, **23**,
    24, 25

zooplankton 22, **22**, 23, **23**, 24, 25
pollution 7, 12, 31, 33, 40–42, **43**,
  44, 45
  oil 31, 40–41, **40**, 44
  sewage 41–2, **41**, 44
  rubbish 42, **42**, **43**

Red Sea **30**, 31

salp 23, **23**
salt water 14, 15, 32, 33, 34
scuba divers 16, 17, **17**, 18, **18**, 30
sea birds 24, 40
sea cucumber 22, 29
sea urchin 27, **27**, 29
seaweed 17, **17**, 26
sessile animals 26
sharks **1**, 8, 15, 21, 24, **24**
sonar 19
starfish 22, 29, 32, **32**
stingray **28**
submersibles 18–19, **19**, 21, 22
sustainability 43

tectonic plates **9**, 10
tides 11
  power from 36, **36**
tourism 31, 32, **43**, 44, **44**
trench 5, 6, 10, 19
tripod fish 22
turtles 11, 15, **15**, 25

USA 6, 32, 38

waves 4, 5, 10
  power from 36
weather 12, 13, **13**
whales 6, 7, 11, 15, 24, 25, **25**,
  38, 39, **39**, 42
whale shark 6, **6**
whaling 38–9, **39**, 45
winds 11